Published by Wildlife Education, Ltd.
12233 Thatcher Court, Poway, California 92064
contact us at: **1-800-477-5034**
e-mail us at: **animals@zoobooks.com**
visit us at: **www.zoobooks.com**

ISBN 1-888153-92-X

Giraffes

Created and Written by
John Bonnett Wexo

Scientific Consultants
Anne Innis Dagg, Ph.D.
*Wildlife Biologist, Consultant
and Freelance Writer*

J. Bristol Foster, Ph.D.
*Ecological Reserves Unit
Ministry of Lands, Parks, and Housing
Victoria, B.C., Canada*

John Harris, Ph.D.
*Department of Paleontology
Los Angeles County Museum of
Natural History*

Contents

Giraffes are the tallest of all land animals. Most of their great height comes from their long necks and long legs. Giraffe necks are so long that the animals can reach high into the trees to feed on leaves. Their legs are so long that they can take huge steps when they walk or run.

Strange as it may seem, the origin of the giraffe's name had nothing to do with the animal's size. It was the giraffe's speed that gave it its name. The word "giraffe" comes from the Arab word *xirapha* (zee-**rah**-fah), which means "the one that walks very fast."

Giraffes live in Africa, but they are only found in certain parts of that continent—usually on tree-dotted plains or in open forests, where the trees are not too close together. They are seldom seen in deserts or in dense forests.

Because they are plant eaters, or *herbivores* (**hur**-buh-vorz), giraffes like to live where there are plenty of trees—their favorite foods are the leaves of trees. But they avoid thick forests, where they can't see approaching lions or other predators and where tangled branches might keep them from running away.

Sometimes giraffes wander great distances in their search for food. They often spend only a few minutes eating at one tree before going on to another. Moving from tree to tree, a giraffe can walk hundreds of miles in a few months.

Most of the animals that live on the African plains must go to a water hole or stream every day to drink. Giraffes go less often. They get much of the water they need from the moisture-laden green leaves and twigs they eat. Water holes are risky places where lions lie in wait, and it is awkward for giraffes to adjust their long legs and lower their heads to drink. A giraffe that can do without a big gulp of water is a safer giraffe.

Groups of giraffes are called herds, although they differ from the herds of most other animals. A giraffe herd can consist of anywhere from 2 to 50 animals, but individuals regularly wander off by themselves or join other herds.

Adult male giraffes are called bulls, adult females are cows, and a young giraffe of either sex is a calf. The oldest giraffe in captivity lived to be 28 years old. In the wild, a few giraffes have been known to live for close to 27 years, but the average lifespan of the giraffe is 10 years.

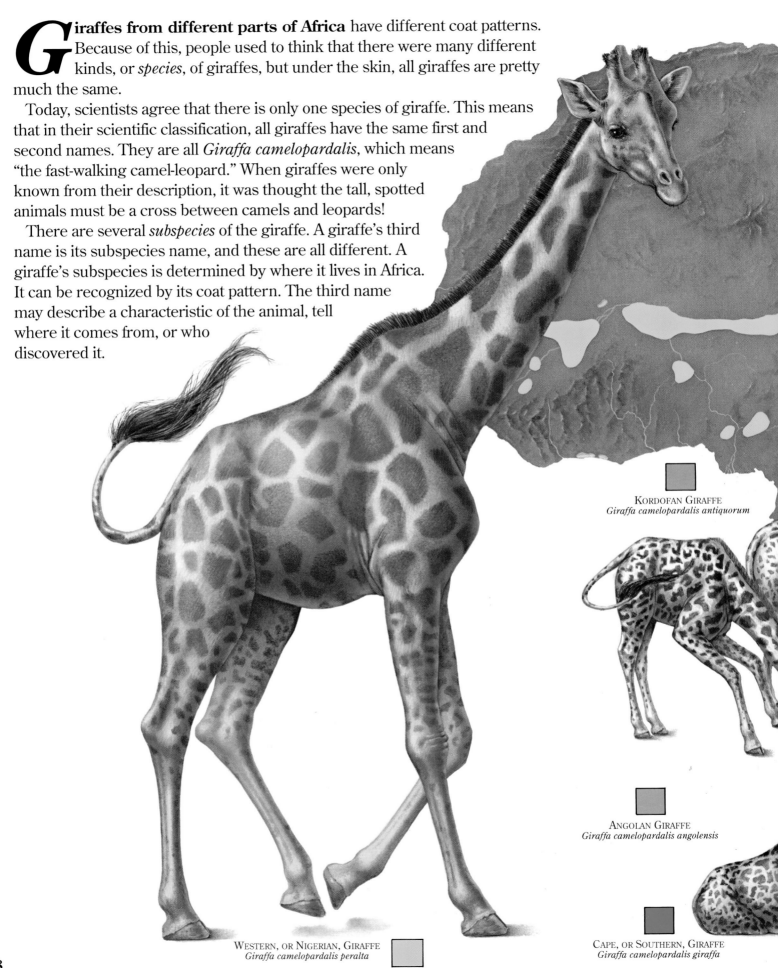

Giraffes from different parts of Africa have different coat patterns. Because of this, people used to think that there were many different kinds, or *species*, of giraffes, but under the skin, all giraffes are pretty much the same.

Today, scientists agree that there is only one species of giraffe. This means that in their scientific classification, all giraffes have the same first and second names. They are all *Giraffa camelopardalis*, which means "the fast-walking camel-leopard." When giraffes were only known from their description, it was thought the tall, spotted animals must be a cross between camels and leopards!

There are several *subspecies* of the giraffe. A giraffe's third name is its subspecies name, and these are all different. A giraffe's subspecies is determined by where it lives in Africa. It can be recognized by its coat pattern. The third name may describe a characteristic of the animal, tell where it comes from, or who discovered it.

KORDOFAN GIRAFFE
Giraffa camelopardalis antiquorum

ANGOLAN GIRAFFE
Giraffa camelopardalis angolensis

WESTERN, OR NIGERIAN, GIRAFFE
Giraffa camelopardalis peralta

CAPE, OR SOUTHERN, GIRAFFE
Giraffa camelopardalis giraffa

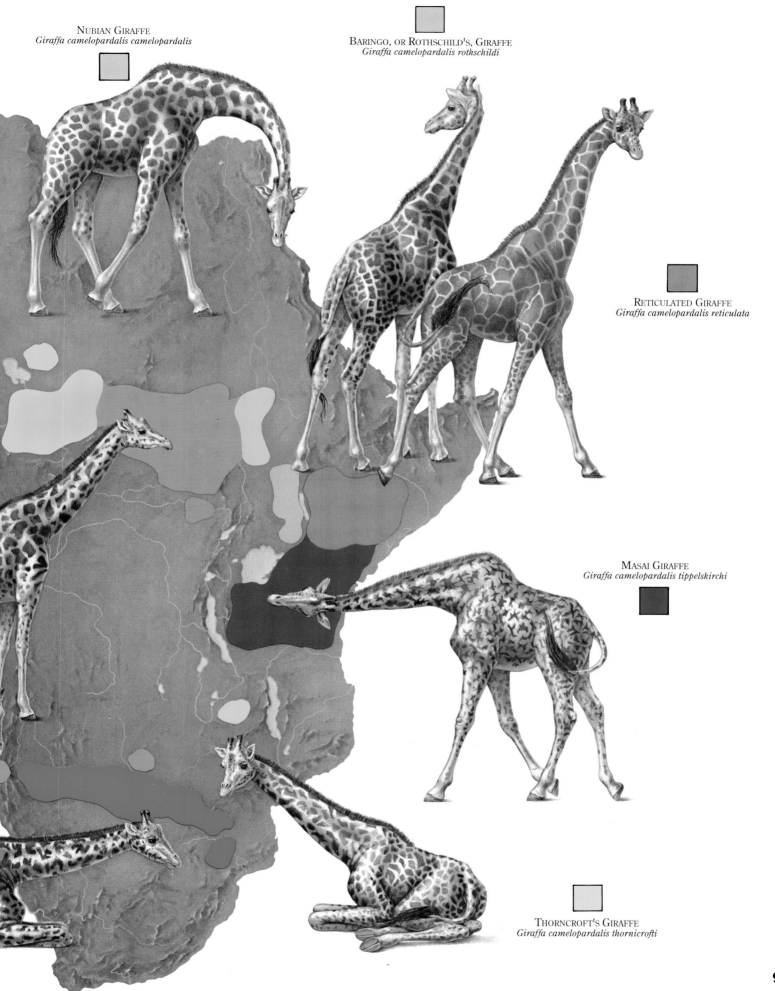

NUBIAN GIRAFFE
Giraffa camelopardalis camelopardalis

BARINGO, OR ROTHSCHILD'S, GIRAFFE
Giraffa camelopardalis rothschildi

RETICULATED GIRAFFE
Giraffa camelopardalis reticulata

MASAI GIRAFFE
Giraffa camelopardalis tippelskirchi

THORNCROFT'S GIRAFFE
Giraffa camelopardalis thornicrofti

Giraffes use the tassels on their tails to swish flies and other insects off their bodies. Each hair in the tassel is 10 to 20 times thicker than a hair on your head.

The neck of a large giraffe can be six feet long. Its tail is about the same length—or longer—if you include the long tassel of hair at the end of the tail.

*E*verything about a giraffe is BIG. Adult male giraffes are usually about 16 feet tall, and they can weigh as much as 3,000 pounds. The largest male on record was more than 19 feet tall. The giraffe's large heart (sometimes two feet long) can pump about 20 gallons of blood every minute. Like cattle and other ruminants, giraffes have four stomachs. A large male eats as much as 75 pounds of food a day. Because a giraffe in the wild gets so much of its moisture from the food it eats, it usually doesn't need to drink large amounts of water. But in captivity, on a hot day, a giraffe can drink 10 gallons of water at one time.

Females are smaller than males—but still very large. An average female reaches 14 to 15 feet, with the largest recorded female standing almost 17 feet tall.

When most animals run, their rear legs do most of the pushing. Giraffes are different. When they run, the front legs do most of the pushing. This is one reason giraffes have such large muscles in their shoulders.

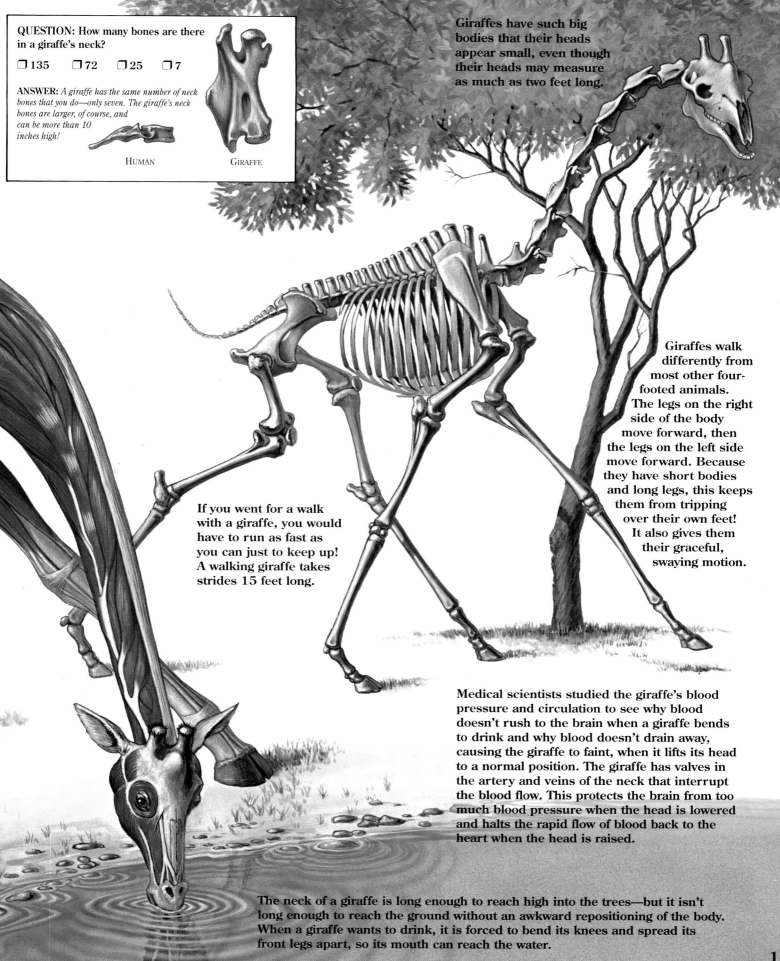

QUESTION: How many bones are there in a giraffe's neck?

□ 135 □ 72 □ 25 □ 7

ANSWER: *A giraffe has the same number of neck bones that you do—only seven. The giraffe's neck bones are larger, of course, and can be more than 10 inches high!*

HUMAN   GIRAFFE

Giraffes have such big bodies that their heads appear small, even though their heads may measure as much as two feet long.

Giraffes walk differently from most other four-footed animals. The legs on the right side of the body move forward, then the legs on the left side move forward. Because they have short bodies and long legs, this keeps them from tripping over their own feet! It also gives them their graceful, swaying motion.

If you went for a walk with a giraffe, you would have to run as fast as you can just to keep up! A walking giraffe takes strides 15 feet long.

Medical scientists studied the giraffe's blood pressure and circulation to see why blood doesn't rush to the brain when a giraffe bends to drink and why blood doesn't drain away, causing the giraffe to faint, when it lifts its head to a normal position. The giraffe has valves in the artery and veins of the neck that interrupt the blood flow. This protects the brain from too much blood pressure when the head is lowered and halts the rapid flow of blood back to the heart when the head is raised.

The neck of a giraffe is long enough to reach high into the trees—but it isn't long enough to reach the ground without an awkward repositioning of the body. When a giraffe wants to drink, it is forced to bend its knees and spread its front legs apart, so its mouth can reach the water.

Giraffes lead placid lives. They have few enemies and appear docile, but they are fully equipped to defend themselves. Lions, leopards, and hyenas attack baby giraffes, but only occasionally do they attempt to kill an adult. A giraffe defends her baby and herself with powerful kicks from both front and rear legs. A giraffe's kick can kill a lion.

Male giraffes sometimes use their heads as weapons. When the sledgehammer head is swung by the muscular neck into a lesser animal (1,000 pounds or more) it can break bones and catapult the unlucky animal through the air. On rare occasions, male giraffes go into head-swinging combat with each other to decide which is the dominant animal.

Given a choice, a giraffe prefers to walk (or run) from trouble. One of the largest and strongest animals on earth is also one of the most peaceful.

The pattern of spots on every giraffe is unique—different from the patterns on all other giraffes. For this reason, scientists are able to use the spot patterns on giraffe necks to tell one giraffe from another. You can do it, too. Look closely at the spots on the giraffe neck at left, then try to find the same pattern on one of the giraffes in the picture above. (Hint: Use the three darker spots at the top of the neck as a guide.)

Giraffes give birth standing up, so the 150-pound calf has a five-foot fall to the ground. After about 15 minutes, the newborn giraffe unravels its long legs and stands to its full height of six feet—taller than many full-grown men and women. During the first week of its life, the calf grows more than an inch a day. By the time it is one year old, it will be almost 10 feet tall. Usually, one giraffe is born at a time. Twins are rare.

Within an hour after it is born, a baby giraffe is able to walk and take milk from its mother. A few days after birth, young giraffes begin to nibble at other food. After the first few months, they continue to nurse briefly twice a day for another year.

The footprints of giraffes are larger than dinner plates. An adult male can have feet 12 inches long and 9 inches wide.

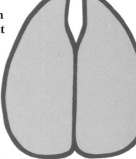

COW FOOT   GIRAFFE FOOT

Many people think that giraffes don't have voices and can't make sounds, just because they have never heard them. Giraffes just don't vocalize very often. They do sometimes moo, bleat, and grunt. When they are alarmed, they snort. The snort isn't an effective alarm signal, though, because other giraffes frequently ignore the sound. Giraffes are just quiet by nature.

Long legs make giraffes good runners and high steppers. A large giraffe can easily step over a six-foot fence, then run off at a speed of 35 miles per hour.

In Africa, giraffes are often seen with little birds on their backs. These are tick birds. They eat ticks and other insects that may attach themselves to a giraffe's skin. This feeds the birds and cleans the giraffe's skin, making the giraffe more comfortable. This mutually beneficial relationship is called *symbiosis*.

Giraffes are like walking lookout towers. Their eyes are so far above the ground that they can usually see what's coming long before other animals see it. In Africa, when a group of giraffes turns to stare in one direction, they may see a lion coming. In a zoo (above), they probably see a keeper coming with food.

Giraffes would rather eat than sleep. In fact, they eat 16 to 20 hours a day. They begin early in the morning and rest during the hottest part of the day. While they rest they may chew some of the food they ate that morning! Giraffes don't do much chewing before they swallow their food. Instead, they later bring small amounts of food back into the mouth and chew it completely before swallowing it again. This is called *ruminating* (**roo**-min-ait-ing) or "chewing cud." Giraffes ruminate several hours a day—usually while they rest.

After their midday rest, giraffes begin to feed again, until after midnight. Then they lie down to rest and ruminate, with their legs curled beneath them and their necks and heads held high. When a giraffe goes into a deep sleep— for about one minute at a time—it curls its neck back and rests its head on its rump. Giraffes sleep no more than 5 to 30 minutes in a 24-hour period.

A giraffe's upper lip and its 18-inch-long tongue are *prehensile*. This means the giraffe can grasp with its lip and its tongue. This grasping ability helps the giraffe strip leaves from branches.

In nature, animals that live in the same area don't usually eat the same kinds of food. Some animals (like zebras) eat grass that is close to the ground. Others (like gerenuks) eat leaves on low bushes. Giraffes, of course, eat leaves high up in the trees. In this way, the animals don't compete directly for food, and there is usually enough for all.

Giraffes are browsers. This means they eat leaves and buds from trees and bushes. They do not usually eat grass. Their favorite food is *acacia* (uh-**kay**-shuh) leaves and twigs. Giraffes seem to ignore the long thorns that protect the trees. They strip the leaves with their lower teeth and avoid most of the thorns.

The "horns" on a giraffe are bony lumps on the skull, covered with skin and hair. They are called *ossicones* (ah-suh-kohnz). Giraffes often have more than two ossicones. As males get older, they develop more bony lumps. Some males have as many as five ossicones.

An adult male's ossicones usually have the hair rubbed off the top. This is because the males use their horns in ritualized combat and sometimes in serious fights. Females and young giraffes have tufts of hair at the tops of their horns.

Young adult male giraffes spar to establish rank with a behavior called "necking." They stand side by side and wrap their necks together. Then they move in slow motion—wrapping, unwrapping, bending, and pushing. This may go on for half an hour before one concedes to the other. During this ritualized "fight," they may rub or bash their horns against each other.

For months after they are born, young giraffes may not go into open country to feed with the adults. Instead, their mothers leave them in a kindergarten with other baby giraffes. Usually, a single female watches over the young giraffes, but sometimes the group of youngsters is left alone in a place with good visibility.

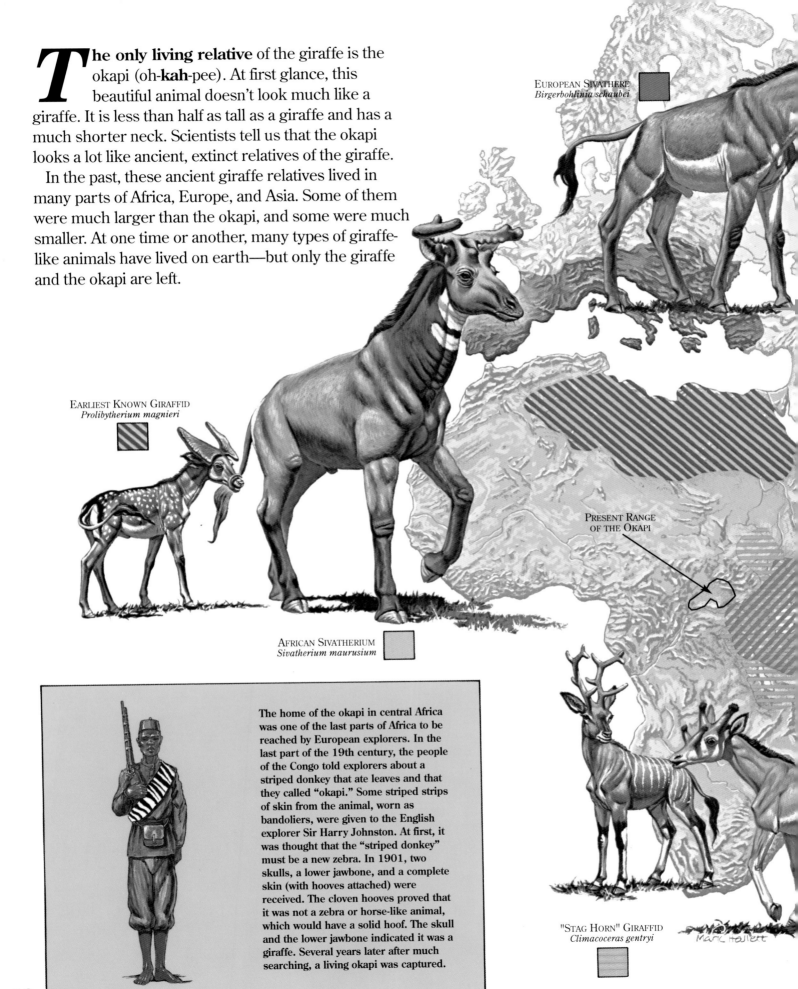

The only living relative of the giraffe is the okapi (oh-**kah**-pee). At first glance, this beautiful animal doesn't look much like a giraffe. It is less than half as tall as a giraffe and has a much shorter neck. Scientists tell us that the okapi looks a lot like ancient, extinct relatives of the giraffe.

In the past, these ancient giraffe relatives lived in many parts of Africa, Europe, and Asia. Some of them were much larger than the okapi, and some were much smaller. At one time or another, many types of giraffe-like animals have lived on earth—but only the giraffe and the okapi are left.

EUROPEAN SIVATHERE
Birgerbohlinia schaubei

EARLIEST KNOWN GIRAFFID
Prolibytherium magnieri

PRESENT RANGE
OF THE OKAPI

AFRICAN SIVATHERIUM
Sivatherium maurusium

"STAG HORN" GIRAFFID
Climacoceras gentryi

The home of the okapi in central Africa was one of the last parts of Africa to be reached by European explorers. In the last part of the 19th century, the people of the Congo told explorers about a striped donkey that ate leaves and that they called "okapi." Some striped strips of skin from the animal, worn as bandoliers, were given to the English explorer Sir Harry Johnston. At first, it was thought that the "striped donkey" must be a new zebra. In 1901, two skulls, a lower jawbone, and a complete skin (with hooves attached) were received. The cloven hooves proved that it was not a zebra or horse-like animal, which would have a solid hoof. The skull and the lower jawbone indicated it was a giraffe. Several years later after much searching, a living okapi was captured.

The okapi and the giraffe, along with all of their ancient relatives, are called giraffids (juh-**raf**-idz). According to the fossil record, the earliest known giraffid lived in North Africa about 15 million years ago. Many of the ancient giraffids had much larger horns than a giraffe or an okapi. The last of the ancient giraffids to die out was probably the Sivatherium shown below. Some scientists believe that this animal did not become extinct until 5,000 years ago. A sculpture (right) created at that time in Iraq seems to show a Sivatherium.

ASIATIC SIVATHERIUM
Sivatherium giganteum

Although the okapi is related to the giraffe, it is different in many ways. It lives in the forest, for instance, and usually lives alone (except for mothers with babies). Females are larger than males, and only young okapis have manes. Instead of spots, an okapi has a dark, velvety coat, with zebra-like stripes on the legs. This color and pattern help to hide the animal in the dark forest.

OKAPI
Okapia johnstoni

"HORN-NOSED" SIVATHERE
Giraffokeryx punjabiensis

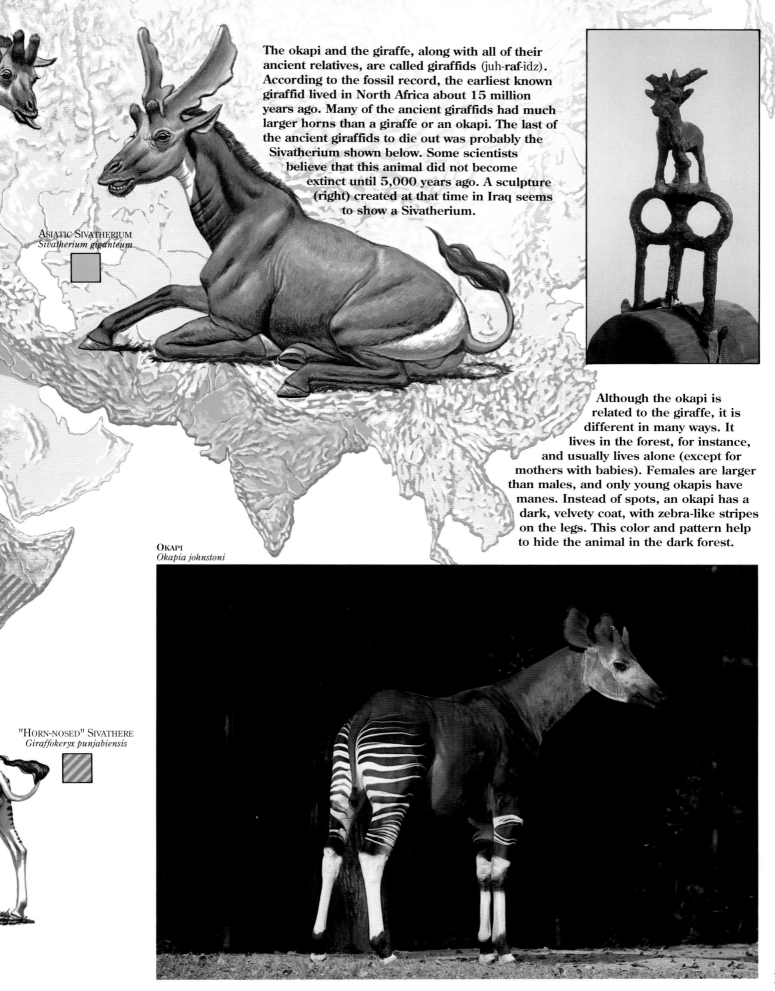

19

People have always admired giraffes. You might say that we humans have always "looked up" to giraffes, because they are so much taller than we are. Like whales and elephants and dinosaurs, their sheer size fills us with wonder and respect. More than that, the odd shape and gentleness of these giants have excited our curiosity.

Long ago, people began trying to explain why giraffes look the way they do. One very old African story said that God made the giraffe after finishing the camel and the leopard. There were some parts left over, so God decided to make an animal that was as big as a camel with spots like a leopard. The ancient Romans and Greeks believed similar stories and called the giraffe a "camel-leopard." And that's how the giraffe got one of its scientific names: *camelopardalis*.

China was the first country to receive a giraffe as a political gift. In 1414, the African kingdom of Malindi presented a giraffe to the Emperor of China. Europeans didn't believe the giraffe existed until the 18th century, when explorers told of this unusual beast. It was the 19th century before giraffes arrived in Europe, where they were sent to royalty.

As long as there have been zoos, giraffes have been popular zoo animals. The first zoo in the world was created 3,500 years ago by Queen Hatshepsut of Egypt. She launched the first animal-collecting expedition—to the Land of Punt—and a giraffe was brought 1,500 miles down the Nile River for the Queen's zoo.

The grace and beauty of giraffes have thrilled people for a very long time. More than 10,000 years ago, an unknown artist painted this scene on the wall of a cave in North Africa.

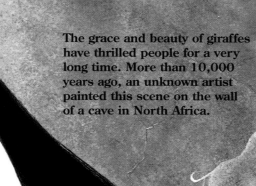

In some parts of Africa, people believe that giraffe tails are lucky. A bracelet or fly whisk made of the hair from a giraffe's tail is supposed to keep its owner healthy and safe from danger. Luckily for giraffes, this belief is dying out.

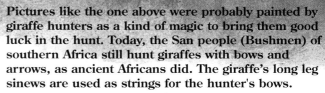

Pictures like the one above were probably painted by giraffe hunters as a kind of magic to bring them good luck in the hunt. Today, the San people (Bushmen) of southern Africa still hunt giraffes with bows and arrows, as ancient Africans did. The giraffe's long leg sinews are used as strings for the hunter's bows.

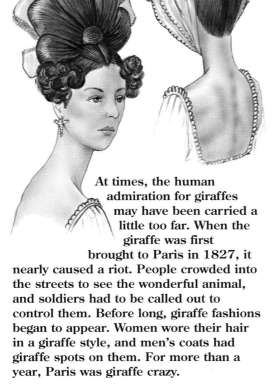

At times, the human admiration for giraffes may have been carried a little too far. When the giraffe was first brought to Paris in 1827, it nearly caused a riot. People crowded into the streets to see the wonderful animal, and soldiers had to be called out to control them. Before long, giraffe fashions began to appear. Women wore their hair in a giraffe style, and men's coats had giraffe spots on them. For more than a year, Paris was giraffe crazy.

21

The future of giraffes is not as dark as the future of many other African animals. For one thing, people really like giraffes and want to help them survive. This was not always the case. Boer settlers in South Africa killed giraffes in great numbers to make bullwhips from the giraffes' tough hide. But giraffes really don't give anyone any reason for hurting them. Giraffes do not bother the cattle and other livestock that people raise. They usually don't eat the crops that people grow.

Giraffes stay pretty much out of people's way and mind their own business.

Unfortunately, it isn't always easy for people to stay out of the way of giraffes. The number of people in Africa grows so fast that humans and giraffes find themselves in competition for the same living space in many places. People need more and more land on which to live and raise food. This means that less and less land is available for the trees that giraffes like to eat and for the giraffes themselves.

The growing number of humans has brought another serious problem with it. There are a great many poor and hungry people in Africa, and hungry people kill giraffes to get the great amount of meat that is on every giraffe. Some illegal hunters, or poachers, still hunt giraffes for their tail hairs to make bracelets, fly whisks, and other tourist items.

Game rangers try to protect giraffes and other animals inside Africa's national parks. Outside the parks, there is usually nobody to protect the wildlife. Many giraffes still live outside the national parks. Someday, though, the only room for giraffes may be inside the parks. Their numbers may be smaller, but they will be safe, and they will survive. For what would Africa be without the stately giraffe moving with grace and dignity over the plains? In the words of the explorer, Samuel Baker, "No one who has merely seen the giraffe in a cold climate can form the least idea of its beauty in its native land."